4 PRACTICES OF LOVING YOUR NEIGHBOR AS YOURSELF
A PERSONAL & COMMUNITY GUIDE

with Brian Mavis, Rick Rusaw, Kevin Colón
& Krista Petty

Copyright © 2017 by Neighboring Life, LLC

Published by Neighboring Life, LLC
10345 Ute Highway, Longmont, CO 80504
neighboringlife.com

Printed in the United States of America.

Library of Congress Cataloging-in-Publication Data is on file at the Library of Congress, Washington, D.C.

ISBN 978-0-9991158-1-7

Unless otherwise indicated, all Scripture passages are taken from Holy Bible, New International Version®, NIV® Copyright ©1973, 1978, 1984, 2011 by Biblica, Inc.® Used by permission. All rights reserved worldwide.

Cover Design by Lonnie Gilbert Designs.

Cover photo by Getty Images.

table of contents

how to use this guide

Jesus said, "Love your neighbor as yourself" (Matthew 22:39). Those five words are filled with power, adventure, challenge and so much more. In those words, we find a way of living this life with others. Those words not only have the power to change others, they have the power to change us. And so, we can't dismiss them. Instead we must embrace them, look deeply into them, study them, reflect on them, find ways to practice them, and allow God to transform us through them.

You will notice throughout this study guide, we have coined a word, neighboring, which encapsulates all of the aspects of what Jesus intended by loving your neighbor as yourself. Neighboring is learning your neighbors name, praying for your neighbor, talking with your neighbor, and even helping them out.

The Neighboring Life is a resource to help you personally reflect and engage in the best thoughts and practices of loving your neighbor. Allow them to sink in and think through them. We recommend going through *The Neighboring Life* with others, so that you can brainstorm with one another, pray together and sharpen one another as you live out the neighboring practices explored in this book.

You can use *The Neighboring Life:*

- as a personal devotion
- in a discipleship or mentoring relationship
- as a family
- in a small group or missional community

THE COMMUNITY EXPERIENCE

At the end of each main section, you will find a community experience. This section is most useful for guiding conversations. Here are the elements you will find within:

Begin by Connecting

Each lesson will open with a few questions to introduce new group members and get the conversation started. This section will also contain a follow up question about the assignment from the previous weeks' meeting (see Challenges for Growth on the next page).

Introduction

Each session begins with a lengthy introduction to explain each of the neighboring principles. Since the group is also watching a video segment, each group member should read the introduction on their own before each meeting. A group member can read a portion of the introduction out loud in the meeting, but there won't be time to read the entire introduction.

Watch the Video

Each lesson features teaching by Rick Rusaw and/or Brian Mavis along with other speakers, which is available on both DVD and streaming video. The group should watch the video when indicated in the lesson prior to the discussion. Space is provided to take notes during the video presentation.

Scripture for Foundation

The scriptures are central to our experience together. Use them all the way through the dialogue. Keep pointing people back to the Bible to answer existing and new questions that may arise.

Questions for Conversation

The questions are designed to lead you into a discussion. Some questions can have several answers or even give room for opinion. Others are more straight forward. Give space for the dialogue. Do not be afraid of silence. Let people have room to think and answer.

Challenges for Growth

Each week you'll have a community challenge. These challenges will stretch you to practice the ways of neighboring. Each week, we recommend you debrief the previous week's challenge. This is such an important part of the journey, we put it right at the beginning of your time together.

Prayer for Strength

W. S. Bowd says, "Prayer is weakness leaning on omnipotence." Neighboring is hard. God is strong. Each week we will be taking time to pray together. Don't skip this part. Don't rush this part. This will be a space for support, for encouragement and for tapping into the only power that can make any of this happen.

Prepare for Next Week

Other than the neighboring activity you choose to try during the week, there is not much home work in this study. To prepare, however, for the next meeting, we recommend reading the introduction to the next lesson on your own before the meeting. As a start to the study, read the introduction to Week 1 now.

FAMILY ON MISSION

For some of us, we live in the context of family and so our neighboring happens as such. If you are a family with kids, this section will help you wrap your minds around what it might look like to love your neighbors together. Special thanks to Craig Wilson and Laurie Bates from the family ministry team of LifeBridge Christian Church for contributing to these sections!

Stories to Inspire

Sprinkled throughout the book, like on the videos, are stories of real people loving their neighbors. Some stories will inspire, and others will challenge. All of them are true life examples of people loving their neighbors as themselves. You are not alone in this journey!

A NOTE FOR COMMUNITY FACILITATORS

First, thank you for being a catalyst for helping people love their neighbors better! As a leader or facilitator of this community experience, you have an important role to play. You will be guiding people through a transformative journey that will help them explore and practice several aspects of neighboring. As you lead, you will need to keep a few things in mind:

- Neighboring is not new. Loving your neighbor was always an intended practice of Jesus' followers.

- Not everyone is on the same page of the neighboring journey. Meet people where they are and help them take their next steps.

- You do not have to be an expert in this process. Lead as a fellow learner. Let people know you are on this journey with them.

There is no commandment greater than these....
(Mark 12:28–31)

week 1:
what matters
most

start by connecting

1. If your group is meeting for the first time or if new members have joined your group, please take a few minutes to introduce yourself and learn a few fun facts about each person in the group.

2. Have everyone in the group give their contact information on the Group Roster on page 123 Just pass one study guide around the room to collect names, phone numbers, and email addresses. The group leader can share this with the rest of the group after the meeting.

3. As your group begins, it's good to start with the Group Agreement on page 121. This will establish the ground rules for your group from when the group will start and end to important group dynamics, like confidentiality.

introduction

Jesus declared "Love God and love your neighbor as yourself" to be the Greatest Commandment. In the book of Mark we have a longer, fuller version of what Jesus said. A teacher of the law asked him, "Of all the commandments, which is the most important?"

Jesus answered:

> The most important one . . . is this: "Hear, O Israel: The Lord our God, the Lord is one. Love the Lord your God with all your heart and with all your soul and with all your mind and with all your strength." The second is this: "Love your neighbor as yourself." There is no commandment greater than these. (Mark 12:28–31)

"Hear, O Israel: The Lord our God, the Lord is one." This is kind of a strange way to begin the answer to the question of what is the greatest commandment. It seems like Jesus is merely warming up until he gets to the real stuff, or worse yet, he begins with math— God is one, not two or twenty or a million. But this statement is no math problem—no mere prelude to the answer. It is part of his answer to the first great commandment and gives greater force to Jesus' answer.

Jesus begins by quoting the Shema (pronounced "shmah"). The Shema is three sections of scripture found in Deuteronomy 6:4-9; 11:13-21; and Numbers 15:37-41 that faithful Jews memorized and repeated twice a day. Jesus would have been taught the Shema as a child, and he would have recited it morning and evening as a vow of obedience to God. And that's the point.

The title Shema comes from the first word of the recitation—"Shema Israel." It is Hebrew for "hear." But this hearing isn't merely auditory; it is about obedience. Not just hearers, but doers of the Word, putting what they hear into practice. How do you show love to God? You obey him. In John 14:15 Jesus says, "If you love me, keep my commands." Later is verses 23 and 24 he says, "Anyone who loves me will obey my teaching. My Father will love them, and we will come to them and make our home with them. Anyone who does not love me will not obey my teaching. These words you hear are not my own; they belong to the Father who sent me."

For many, the word obey sounds like a drag—going against what we really want. But to God and Jesus, to obey is to live the way we were created to live. John writes, "This is how we know that we love the children of God: by loving God and carrying out his commands. In fact, this is love for God: to keep his commands. And his commands are not burdensome, for everyone born of God overcomes the world." (1 John 5:2-4). What matters most? Our obedience to the command to love both God and our neighbor. Obedience and love are both foundational and our motivation for everything else we are about to learn in the next six weeks. Love God and love your neighbor as yourself—you and your neighbor were made for this!

Show me!

If you are a parent, a boss, a co-worker, a caregiver or in position of authority, you know full well that obedience is not in the hearing, it is in the doing. If you asked your son to move the laundry from the washer to the dryer, the only way you know he obeyed your command is to see the laundry in the actual dryer.

James 1:22- 25 says:

> Do not merely listen to the word, and so deceive yourselves. Do what it says. Anyone who listens to the word but does not do what it says is like someone who looks at his face in a mirror and, after looking at himself, goes away and immediately forgets what he looks like. But whoever looks intently into the perfect law that gives freedom, and continues in it—not forgetting what they have heard, but doing it— they will be blessed in what they do.

How often do we forget to show God we have heard him by acting on his word? And as James points out, acting on what we hear is not just for God's benefit, it is for ours! We will be "blessed" in what we do.

The Great Commandment taught by Jesus wasn't the great suggestion, like 10 tips for a better life. Let's examine it again, this time from Matthew 22:37-40:

> *One of them, an expert in the law, tested him with this question: "Teacher, which is the greatest commandment in the Law?"*

> *Jesus replied: "Love the Lord your God with all your heart and with all your soul and with all your mind. This is the first and greatest commandment. And the second is like it: Love your neighbor as yourself. All the Law and the Prophets hang on these two commandments."*

Did you catch that? Jesus said that everything that has ever been commanded and taught about the Kingdom of God hinges on these two commandments.
What a relief, actually! If we can just concentrate on these

WHAT?	WHO?	HOW?
LOVE	GOD	WITH ALL YOUR HEART, SOUL, MIND (AND STRENGTH Mark 12:30)
LOVE	YOUR NEIGHBOR	AS YOURSELF

two commandments we can rest assured that everything else will be taken care of. Following Jesus is not about a bunch of endless rules and regulations, it's simply about love. Yes, it's easier said than done, but it is certainly simple enough. Give love. Receive love. Think about love. Act in love. Focus on love. Make all of your life revolve around love.

But the Truth Is...

Many of us have said, "YES" to loving God. We have come to a place of belief. Our belief has encouraged us to make our lives more and more like Christ's. We have learned the lessons. We have memorized the verses. We have read our scriptures. We have joined a church community...

The question is, "Have you said, 'YES' to loving your neighbors? At first, you may think, "Well, of course!" But ask yourself the question one more time. Have you said, "YES" to God that you will make your life about loving your neighbors? This is a crucial question and it demands a decision by each one of us. And just for clarity, this is not a decision that your pastor makes for you or your church makes on your behalf. This is your decision.

Just as each one of us must make a personal decision to love God, each person must make a personal decision about loving our neighbors. This is a commitment you make. It's a vow. It's a stake in the ground that marks obedience to the Great Commandment... This is the kind of decision that aligns you with the heart of God.

Yes, Love Your Literal Neighbor

A "neighbor" in the scriptures is best defined as anyone in close proximity to you that has need. By that definition, anyone could be your neighbor. Unfortunately, many of us use that wide definition of neighbor, then go on to pick and choose who we are going to love and who we are not going to love. We take matters into our hands based on our preferences or conveniences, which was never Jesus' intention.

Jesus' example to us was being fully present wherever he went. He paid attention and met the needs of the people right in front of him. Later, Jesus' encouragement to the disciples as he first sent them out was to start loving people right where they were. They were to start the mission in Jerusalem before they took the message any further (Acts 1:8). In the same way, we cannot neglect the people right next door. God put us in our neighborhoods for a reason. God put our neighbors next to us for a reason, as well. Obey God right where you live.

Ok, but HOW do we get better at loving our neighbors?

Sometimes we need a plan to head in the right direction. As you'll hear Brian share on the video, he thought he would be a better dad. Here are a few more details to that story.

The thought of being a better dad had been going through his mind for weeks when his two girls were elementary school age. He wasn't a bad dad. He just imagined he would be better than he was. He realized that good intentions weren't good enough. He needed a plan. Businesses had plans to be profitable. Sports teams had plans on how to win games. He needed a plan to be a better dad. But the plan needed to be simple. It needed to be something easily remembered. So, he came up with three habits he would do regularly for and with his girls. He used words that rhymed so it would be easy to remember them.
The first and most fundamental practice would be to **STAY**

in his girls' world. He admits being wrapped up in his world. Like many of us, Brian's mind was on work. His rest was focused on watching sports. Staying wasn't just about being physically present; it was about being emotionally and mentally present. It was about being a student of his children, learning who God made them to be. It was about listening. It was about being interested. It was about doing things like getting on the floor and playing dolls with them.

The second action was to **PRAY** for his girls. He did pray for his girls, but he needed to make it even more of a priority. Consistency was key. He immediately discovered he could also pray better by praying more specifically for them because he had practiced staying in their world. He knew what was going on in their lives, so he could be a better intercessor.

The third habit was to speak into their lives, in other words, **SAY**. He wasn't just to listen but to speak. He wanted to tell them every day he loved them. He wanted to explain to them what Mavis family values are. He wanted them to grow in their understanding of the love of God.

After practicing these for a few weeks, God showed him a habit he had overlooked. Brian and his youngest daughter were goofing around, and she said, "Daddy, my favorite of you is when you're silly!" That's when he realized the importance of regular **PLAY**. Play is serious business in the life of kids, and it is our loss when we don't also play as adults.

He tweaked the order of the words a bit, and came up with four habits of being a better dad: **STAY, PRAY, PLAY, SAY**. Brian has found that these habits can be applied to ANY relationship. Use them to deepen your relationships with your kids, parents, siblings, spouse, coworkers, boss, employees, friends, boyfriend, girlfriend, classmates, teammates—anyone in your sphere of influence.

Of course, the focus of this book is specifically applied to loving your neighbors—those people who live near you, because we want to get better at what Jesus said matters most. Over the next several weeks you will explore each of these simple practices in greater detail. It is our hope that these practices will move from words on a page to a way of life drawing you closer to God, your family and, of course, your neighbors.

STAY | PRAY | PLAY | SAY

watch the video

As a group, watch the short video teaching segments and take notes in the space provided below.

scripture for foundation

Read 2 John 1:4-6.

It has given me great joy to find some of your children walking in the truth, just as the Father commanded us. And now, dear lady, I am not writing you a new command but one we have had from the beginning. I ask that we love one another. And this is love: that we walk in obedience to his commands. As you have heard from the beginning, his command is that you walk in love.

questions for conversation

Before diving into the rest of the study, assess yourself and your neighborhood. There are no wrong answers here! You can do this on your own or if in a small group, gather in groups of 2 or 3 to share your answers.

1. Before today, how did you view the Greatest Commandment—love God and love your neighbor as yourself? In what ways do you think you actively obey this command? How are you walking in love?

_____

_____

_____

_____

_____

_____

2. STAY: How long have you lived in your current home and how many neighbor's names do you know?

_____

_____

_____

_____

3. PRAY: Do you know any of your neighbor's hopes, dreams or hurts that you could be praying about?

_____

_____

_____

_____

4. PLAY: In what ways do people in your neighborhood play together?

_____

_____

_____

_____

_____

5. SAY: Have you ever shared any part of your life story with a neighbor?

_____

_____

_____

_____

6. If you are in a group, gather back together, and discuss any realizations you had about God, yourself or your neighborhood.

_____

_____

_____

_____

7. As the meeting ends, think of other people who would benefit from this study. Pray about an opportunity to invite them to the next group meeting.

_____

_____

_____

_____

prayer for strength

God, you are already present and working in our neighborhoods. In your Word, you promise that you have gone before us and "set eternity in the human heart" which includes our neighbors (Ecclesiastes 3:11). Open our eyes to see your goodness, to see how you love each of us and how you already love our families and neighbors.

challenge for growth

Choose one challenge from this section to try out this week. Remember, you will report back to the group next week.

We are all called to obey the Greatest Commandment. It is a commandment. But when it comes to the other practices, we are all wired differently. Which of the practices is most appealing to you? Rank the following from 1-4. A "1" would be your preferred or natural neighboring practice. A "4" which would be the practice you probably prefer to do the least. Write the number to the left of each practice.

_____ **STAY:** I live to get to know people. I'm a good listener. I enjoy hearing stories. I don't like for people to feel alone.

_____ **PRAY:** I like to pray for others. I see people's needs. I know people's needs. I hope for God's blessings on my neighbors and friends.

_____ **PLAY:** I like to bring people together. I like to have fun. Throwing parties, playing games, enjoying a good meal with friends makes me come alive.

_____ **SAY:** I love to talk about spiritual things. I feel comfortable telling the story of God to others as well as my own story of faith. I like getting people together to talk about God and the Bible.

You may see glimpses of yourself in all four of these areas, but usually one will rise to the top as your primary and more natural way of neighboring. Your primary neighboring approach will be your lead step. As you move into your neighboring journey, you'll learn and grow in the other areas. Talk with someone about your areas of strength and weakness in neighboring this week.

Pick one of the following things to do over the course of the next week. Be prepared to share with the group how you met this challenge.

- Crawl : Learn a neighbor's name.
- Walk : Bring the neighbor's trash can in for them.
- Run : Help your neighbor with some task or ask them to help you.

family on mission

Learning your neighbors' names is a great
step to loving them. Involve your kids in the
conversation of who lives near you. And, what
about your neighbors' dogs? Make a family
challenge to not only learn neighbors' names,
but the names of their pets, too!

JACOB & MARY ALICE: AN UNLIKELY PAIR

Ever since his wife's death, 80-year-old Jacob called his neighbor, Mary Alice, regularly. Somehow Mary Alice had broken the ice with this self-proclaimed "crotchety old Jewish man who doesn't make friends easily." The two were quite a pair in the neighborhood: a mom of two teenagers chatting the ear off the grumpy old man.

When Jacob's number came up on caller ID, she answered it, but on this evening, when she picked up the phone Jacob wasn't talking but she could hear difficulty in his breathing. Rushing over to his house, she found Jacob at the bottom of the stairs and quickly called 911. As the paramedic in the ambulance, emergency room receptionist, technicians drawing blood, and the doctor all asked her, "Are you his daughter?"

"No, I am just his neighbor" she answered every time, as she kept Jacob calm and answered their questions about his past medical history. As Mary Alice left the emergency room after Jacob was fully stabilized, the doctor asked her with a smile, "Will you be MY neighbor?" [1]

---

prepare for next week

Prior to the next group meeting, read the
Week 2 introduction on your own before the meeting.

"Simply put, the gospel and the call to Gospel Neighboring propels us to be present with our neighbors in a way that is now set apart (holy) rather than nonchalant."
—Andy Stager

week 2:
stay

start by connecting

1. If new members have joined your group, take time to introduce yourself.

2. Share how last week's challenge went. What did you learn about yourself or someone else through that challenge? Where did you see God in your neighborhood this past week?

In Christ

You may have heard of the concept of being "in Christ." We have scripture that encourages us to abide in Christ or to remain in Christ. In John 15:4, Jesus says, "Remain in me, as I also remain in you. No branch can bear fruit by itself; it must remain in the vine. Neither can you bear fruit unless you remain in me." In other words, the scriptures tell us that we should stick with Jesus and stay connected with him. In the context of that relationship, we find everything we need to make our relationship with him flourish.

It's the same with our earthly relationships. There is a certain level of staying connected that is required to maintain and grow our relationships. We simply cannot build relationships apart from a steady stream of regular interactions and conversations. As we learned in lesson 1, STAY is all about those connections. STAY is about being not just physically present, but also emotionally and mentally present.

Live "Garage Door Up"

Have you heard the sociological term cocooning? It was popularized in the 1980s by marketing consultant Faith Popcorn. She used her marketing to name different kinds of cocooning, like home-based cocooning, which was typified by watching movies at home instead of going to the theater. Another is wandering cocooning, which was illustrated by people walking in town while plugged into earphones. But since the 1990s cocooning has gotten on steroids—it's called super cocooning now. People are home more and plugged in—visually and audibly—more than ever.

Super cocooning is making us less social said analyst Michael Greeson of the Diffusion Group, a media research group. "With all the information and entertainment at arm's reach at home, why get out and meet up with a friend when you can chat on Facebook? Why go shopping for a book at Barnes & Noble when you can search through a virtually unlimited bookstore like Amazon and never leave your couch?" [2] It appears we are now living in an age where we expect more from technology and less from relationships.

In contrast to living life super cocooned, Drew Depler calls it living with the garage door up. Unfortunately, when some of us live with the garage door up, the dog runs out and leaves reminders on neighbors' lawns and car tires! Still you get the idea.

It's virtually a competitive sport to see how quickly you can pull up to your house, hit the garage door opener, drive into the garage, and close the door. Living garage door up is countercultural. It is a deliberate decision and an attitude toward life. This outward physical act is a great symbol, and affects our hearts to live life open to our neighbors.

Learn Names and More

In the video, Rick will challenge us to fill out the block map, answering these three questions:

- What are your neighbors' names?
- What is something you know about them?
- What is some hurt, hope or dream that they have?

Take time to do that now.

DO YOU KNOW YOUR NEIGHBORS' NAMES, HISTORY, HOPES AND HURTS?

_____   _____   _____

_____   _____   _____

_____   _____   _____

                                          _____

_____   **YOU**   _____

_____

                                          _____

_____   _____   _____

_____   _____   _____

_____   _____   _____

It feels great when someone remembers your name, doesn't it? You know why? Because hardly anyone remembers! If you can just give your neighbors the gift of learning and remembering their names you have made a huge step to love them. It's really that easy! Watch what changes when you address your neighbor by their names. You will be amazed.

Frederick L. Collins once said, "There are two types of people—those who walk into a room and say: 'Here I am!' and those who walk into a room and say: 'There you are.'" If there is one principle about the value and practice of staying, it is to work more on being interested than interesting. Of course, by being interested, your neighbors will think you are interesting. Staying is about loving your neighbors by learning about your neighbors. It's not just about physically staying around; it's about staying attuned and staying interested.

Love Where You Live

Visualize your neighborhood. Go up and down the street in your mind and think of each home. If you live in an apartment, think of the various doors you walk by. Did you know this is your mission field? In many ways, you may be the only human representation of Jesus any of the people in those homes experience.

Acts 17:26 says: "From one man he made all the nations, that they should inhabit the whole earth; and he marked out their appointed times in history and the boundaries of their lands." Acts gives us the idea that God put you where you live for a reason. He knew where you would live, even if it was for a season. There is purpose in the place you live. Your home is the very place where the Greatest Commandment can be put into practice!

When you view your neighborhood as your mission, things drastically change. You may want to hang out there more: STAY. The way you see people, the way you talk to people, the way you serve people...it all changes! God has marked out these days for you to be present and love your neighbors like he would love them if he lived where you live.

Jesus Modeled This for Us

In *Moving Back into the Neighborhood*, Alan Roxburgh wrote: "Jesus is shown to us in the ordinariness of birth, family, place and time. In Jesus, God is always turning up in the ordinariness of the everyday, the local and the regular rhythms of life. Have you noticed the stories Jesus told about who God is and how we know God? These are stories about a woman cleaning her house, a man plowing a field, someone walking from one place to the next, and people who are just hungry and want some food. . . .

Look at how non-spiritual most of them are by our categories of spiritual." [3] Jesus did a number of extraordinary things, of course, but he also did simple, relatable things. The practice of STAY does not have to be a burden. It is seeing God in the ordinary.

JESUS . . .

. . . asked for a drink of water.

. . . attended a wedding.

. . . was a guest at someone's house.

. . . grieved with friends.

. . . told stories, even jokes.

. . . went fishing.

. . . made breakfast on the beach for his friends.

. . . threw raging parties.

. . . gave his friends nicknames like Rock and Sons of Thunder.

. . . prayed for his friends.

. . . called them by name.

. . . shared his life.

. . . made wine.

. . . visited the sick.

. . . saw people and their potential.

. . . even during his worst moments, he blessed his neighbor.

He was touchable, authentic, and available. He was a best friend and the best neighbor. How can you follow the examples of Jesus presented above?

watch the video

As a group, watch the short video teaching segments and take notes in the space provided below.

scripture for foundation

Read the following Scriptures. Pay attention to Jesus' connection with humankind.

Luke 7:36-50:
[Note: Simon mentioned in this passage is Simon, the Pharisee, not Simon Peter, Jesus' disciple.]

> *When one of the Pharisees invited Jesus to have dinner with him, he went to the Pharisee's house and reclined at the table. A woman in that town who lived a sinful life learned that Jesus was eating at the Pharisee's house, so she came there with an alabaster jar of perfume. As she stood behind him at his feet weeping, she began to wet his feet with her tears. Then she wiped them with her hair, kissed them, and poured perfume on them.*

> *When the Pharisee who had invited him saw this, he said to himself, "If this man were a prophet, he would know who is touching him and what kind of woman she is—that she is a sinner."*

> *Jesus answered him, "Simon, I have something to tell you."*

> *"Tell me, teacher," he said.*

> *"Two people owed money to a certain moneylender. One owed him five hundred denarii, and the other fifty. Neither of them had the money to pay him back, so he forgave the debts of both. Now which of them will love him more?"*

Simon replied, "I suppose the one who had the bigger debt forgiven."

"You have judged correctly," Jesus said.

Then he turned toward the woman and said to Simon, "Do you see this woman? I came into your house. You did not give me any water for my feet, but she wet my feet with her tears and wiped them with her hair. You did not give me a kiss, but this woman, from the time I entered, has not stopped kissing my feet. You did not put oil on my head, but she has poured perfume on my feet. Therefore, I tell you, her many sins have been forgiven—as her great love has shown. But whoever has been forgiven little loves little."

Then Jesus said to her, "Your sins are forgiven."

The other guests began to say among themselves, "Who is this who even forgives sins?"

Jesus said to the woman, "Your faith has saved you; go in peace."

John 10:3

The gatekeeper opens the gate for him, and the sheep listen to his voice. He calls his own sheep by name and leads them out.

John 10:14, 15

I am the good shepherd; I know my sheep and my sheep know me— just as the Father knows me and I know the Father—and I lay down my life for the sheep.

questions for conversation

1. In Luke 7, the Pharisee saw the woman as a sinner. How did Jesus see this woman? How do you think Jesus sees you? Based on Jesus' example, how should we see others?

_____

_____

_____

_____

_____

2. Jesus not only heard the Pharisee's opinion of the woman, he also knew his heart. Rather than chastising him, Jesus used this incident as a teachable moment. When are you tempted to straighten someone out who differs from you? How could you take that moment to help the person grow instead?

_____

_____

_____

_____

_____

3. What are the best ways to make natural and genuine connections with your neighbors?

_____

_____

_____

_____

4. What are the best ways to keep those connections going?

_____

_____

_____

_____

_____

5. Being aware and simply noticing is so important in loving our neighbors. How can we be more aware of our neighbors?

_____

_____

_____

_____

_____

6. Rick made a commitment to connect with a neighbor if they were outside every time he came home from work. Right now, in your meeting, go back to the Block Map on page 32 and fill it in for your neighborhood. Your house is at the center of the block, then fill in as much information as you can about the neighbors who live around you. If your neighborhood is configured differently, then make the map work for your neighborhood, apartment building, rural setting, or wherever you live.

_____

_____

_____

_____

_____

7. Each group member should take responsibility for the group by taking a role in the group meeting. Members can host the group in their homes, bring refreshments, lead a portion of the discussion, or lead the entire discussion. Locate the Group Calendar on page 124 and ask everyone to sign up to do something in one of the upcoming group meetings.

_____

_____

_____

_____

_____

prayer for strength

Pray for each other in the areas of awareness and action. Pray that God will direct our steps and show us what our next steps should be with our neighbors. Pray for our hearts to shift in love for our neighbors.

Pray for God's eyes and ears so that we can see people as he sees them and listen to people like he hears them.

challenge for growth

Choose one challenge from this section to try out this week. Remember, you will report back to the group next week.

James 1:19 says "Everyone should be quick to listen, slow to speak..." This week, practice being more present in your relationships, especially with your neighbors. Listen more. Talk less. Listen to empathize with people around you, not to form a response. Pick one of the following challenges and be prepared to share your experience with the group next week.

- **Crawl**: Learn another neighbor's name.
- **Walk**: Literally walk! Take a long walk with neighboring intentions. Walk slower. Stop and visit. Find out some basic facts like how long they've lived in the neighborhood or where they lived before.
- **Run**: Invite a neighbor over for coffee. Make an intentional effort to talk less and listen more to your neighbor.

family on mission

Involve your kids in planning a get-together with your neighbors. Who would they like to invite? What would they like to do? Kids are creative and are often the best connectors! Inviting a family over for dinner or games is a fun, non-threatening way to get to know them better.

DON'S STORY: MY SUITCASE WAS KILLING MY NEIGHBORHOOD

There was a time when I traveled almost weekly as a consultant. I am so glad I don't travel as much anymore, because my suitcase was killing my neighborhood.

My best friend is my neighbor Miguel. Miguel and his wife, Teresa, have raised five children and grandchildren in a one-bedroom apartment. We are guys. We like standing and talking in the yard and looking in holes together. Our backgrounds are really, really different, but we like the same stuff: planting things and fiddling with little projects. He calls me "Neighbor." Of all the English words he knows, neighbor is one of them. He's never called me Don.

I know more about Jesus because I know my neighbors, who exemplify him so much more than I. I see Miguel, the foreigner, and how hard he works and cares for his family. My image of who Jesus is changed because of him. Jesus looks a whole lot more like Miguel than me. He's a saint for the sacrifices he has made so his family can have a better life. If God hadn't prompted me to slow down and have conversations with him, I would have missed that.

—Don Simmons, California

prepare for next week

Prior to the next group meeting, read the Week 3 introduction on your own before the meeting.

"Prayer does not fit us for the greater work;
prayer is the greater work."
—Oswald Chambers

week 3:
pray

start by connecting

1. What is something you recently asked for? How did it turn out?

2. Share how last week's challenge went. What did you learn about yourself or someone else through that challenge? Where did you see God in your neighborhood this past week?

Open Eyes

At the base of your head is a soft spot. Inside that soft spot is a bundle of nerves. That bundle of nerves is called the reticular activator, which acts as a filter. Throughout each day we are flooded with stimuli: sights and sounds. The only way we survive and manage that flood of information and stimuli is for some things to be filtered out. Our brain is trained to open windows for us so some things get in and other things are left out. For example, if you like horses, you will recognize horses wherever you go. Or when you buy a new car, you suddenly see that type of car everywhere you go.

Actually, all that happened is that you opened a window—a space in your brain—for something it had previously filtered out. God designed us that way: to filter the stimuli around us. Here is what happens when we begin to pray: God opens a window in our brain and we begin to see things we didn't see before. The apostle Paul wrote, "I pray that the eyes of your heart may be enlightened" (Ephesians 1:18) and "I urge, then, first of all, that petitions, prayers, intercession and thanksgiving be made for all people" (1 Timothy 2:1). That would include our neighbors, right?

Start by Praying for Yourself

One of the essentials to prayer is to make sure our hearts are right before the Lord. Start by asking God to examine your heart. Are you doing okay? Is your relationship with Jesus alright? Is your heart ready to love others? What do you feel in your heart for your neighbors? Do you have reservations about loving them? Honest conversation with God about your life and your heart is a crucial process.

After the prayer of examination comes the prayer of transformation. Once you have good assessment of where your heart is, you can start asking God to change you. Pray for your heart to expand for your neighbors. Ask God to give you compassion for them. Pray that God would give you eyes to see your neighbor's needs and give you the resources to love your neighbors well.

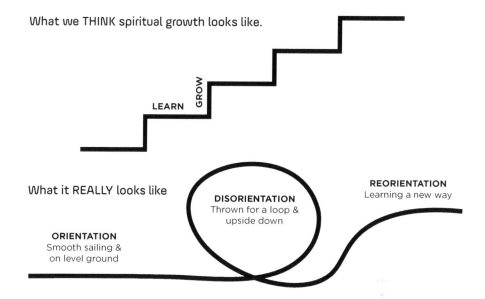

What we THINK spiritual growth looks like.

GROW

LEARN

What it REALLY looks like

DISORIENTATION
Thrown for a loop &
upside down

REORIENTATION
Learning a new way

ORIENTATION
Smooth sailing &
on level ground

Neighboring is not always barbeques and playing catch in the yard. Neighboring can stretch us. Learning to love those who are not like you takes a lot of maturity, sacrifice, and courage.

Eric observed, "It's easier to love humanity as a whole, than to love one's neighbor." In the broad sense, we might be good with loving people, but in a specific sense, that's not so easy to do. Not everybody is somebody we want to care for, much less love. But aren't those the very relationships that grow us closer to God and others?

In the video, Brian will talk about how love is sometimes loopy. It is in the times where we get a disoriented in a relationship that God walks with us to orient us to a new way of love and grace. God is always trying to disciple us, including and especially in our relationships. Prayer should be a foundational practice as we move through different experiences and relationships. We look to God to orient us to his ways and his love.

Get More Specific in Your Prayers!

Many of us have prayed for years for a loved one to come to know Jesus, but it appears absolutely zero, zip, nada has happened. But it's not because God doesn't want our loved ones to trust in him. Maybe our prayers need to be more specific in order to be answerable and actionable and small enough for us to have faith to see it. Brian shares this story about the power of praying specifically:

Some years ago, my wife and I (Brian Mavis) had neighbors across the back ally. We would wave and say "Hi," but that was about it. I had heard through the grapevine that their young son had died before we moved into the neighborhood. I also knew they were sports fans because they watched sports on their television in the backyard while in their hot tub. My heart broke for their deep loss, and I prayed for them to know the peace and healing of God, but nothing happened.

I decided to pray a small, specific prayer. It was a Saturday, and I prayed that God would give me Denver Broncos tickets to give to them. Keep in mind, this had never happened to me before. The next day at church, someone came up to me and said, "Brian, I have a couple of Broncos tickets for today's game. Do you want them?"

Of course I wanted them. I was blown away. I was able to give my neighbors a couple of tickets, and that opened up a new relationship for me to continue to pray small prayers and build on that.

Some Christians believe in prayer. They believe prayer is something they must do, but they don't believe prayer will really change anything. Other Christians BELIEVE in PRAYER. These followers of Jesus realize that prayer is a gift from God to his people. They believe that their prayers actually reach the ears of God and that he will do something about them... James 5:16 says that the prayer of a righteous person can accomplish much. Prayer may indeed be the linchpin in loving our neighbors. Talking to God on behalf of our neighbors cannot be underestimated and certainly cannot be overlooked. If you want to engage and love your neighbors, make sure to PRAY!

Bless Them!

Starting with Abraham, God's family is a family of blessing. Abraham was promised by God that his family would grow into a great nation and that nation would be a blessing to all the other nations. This blessing extends from our homes to the whole world. As you pray for your neighbors, speak prayers of blessings over them. Let your words be filled with blessings for their lives, their jobs, their families, their property, their friendships...everything. That might mean praying for football tickets, like Brian did. Ask God for the very best for them, so much so that they cannot ignore his goodness in their lives!

watch the video

As a group, watch the short video teaching segments and take notes in the space provided below.

Ask and Get.
Matthew 7:7

> *Ask and it will be given to you; seek and you will find; knock and the door will be opened to you.*

Powerful prayers get powerful results.
James 5:13-18

> *Is anyone among you in trouble? Let them pray. Is anyone happy? Let them sing songs of praise. Is anyone among you sick? Let them call the elders of the church to pray over them and anoint them with oil in the name of the Lord. And the prayer offered in faith will make the sick person well; the Lord will raise them up. If they have sinned, they will be forgiven. Therefore confess your sins to each other and pray for each other so that you may be healed. The prayer of a righteous person is powerful and effective.*

Elijah was a human being, even as we are. He prayed earnestly that it would not rain, and it did not rain on the land for three and a half years. Again he prayed, and the heavens gave rain, and the earth produced its crops.

Have confidence that God hears.
1 John 5:14-15

> *This is the confidence we have in approaching God: that if we ask anything according to his will, he hears us. And if we know that he hears us— whatever we ask—we know that we have what we asked of him.*

Pray for those who are tough to pray for.
Matthew 5:43-45

> *"You have heard that it was said, 'Love your neighbor and hate your enemy.' But I tell you, love your enemies and pray for those who persecute you, that you may be children of your Father in heaven. He causes his sun to rise on the evil and the good, and sends rain on the righteous and the unrighteous.*

Pray for more helpers.
Luke 10:2

> *He told them, "The harvest is plentiful, but the workers are few. Ask the Lord of the harvest, therefore, to send out workers into his harvest field.*

The Holy Spirit prays for us.
Romans 8:26

> *In the same way, the Spirit helps us in our weakness. We do not know what we ought to pray for, but the Spirit himself intercedes for us through wordless groans.*

questions for conversation

Make sure to leave time for praying and not just talking about prayer this week.

1. Why do you think praying for your neighbors is such an important habit in loving them?

    _____

    _____

    _____

2. What are some ways you could pray for your neighbors? Think of as many as you can. (Hint: How would you like people to pray for you?)

    _____

    _____

    _____

3. According to Romans 8:26, when you can't think of how to pray for someone, what can you do?

    _____

    _____

    _____

4. There are times when God asks us to be the answer to the prayers for our neighbors. How do you do that? How do you know? Can anyone share an example of this happening to you?

_____

_____

_____

_____

5. What can you do to remind yourself to pray for your neighbors?

_____

_____

_____

_____

6. How can you pray for each other as you engage in praying and loving your neighbors?

_____

_____

_____

_____

challenge for growth

Choose one challenge from this section to try out this week. Remember, you will report back to the group next week.

Keep some notes on what is about to happen in the seven days. Be prepared to share with the group next week.

- **Crawl** : Pick a neighbor, any neighbor, and pray for them for the next seven days. Notice what prayers you pray. Ask God to give you prayers for your neighbors. Write your neighbor's name here:

  _____

- **Walk** : Pray for your neighbors every time they come to mind. The whispers of God keep us connected and focused. When God reminds you of people, it is not arbitrary; it is intentional and purposeful. Ask God if there is anything you need to do.

- **Run** : Be the answer. In the scriptures, the community of Jesus had a bent for meeting needs. They sold their possessions to provide for those in need. They gave money. They took people in. They shared food. They looked after the sick. They welcomed the lonely. They prayed for healing. They did all they could to show the love of Jesus to others. If there was something they could do, they did it. They were the answers to the prayer of their neighbors. That is powerful prayer, right there!

prayer for strength

Break into groups of 2 or 3 for prayer. Praying for our neighbors in so important. Praying for each other.

Pray for each other in these areas:

*   Gaining a heart for our neighbors.

*   Moving from duty of prayer to the privilege of prayer for our neighbors.

*   Increasing compassion and care for our neighbors.

*   That god would help us to listen to him on behalf of our neighbors.

*   That we would be more and more aware of when we need to be the answer to our neighbor's prayers.

family on mission

As you focus on one neighbor to pray for this week, ask your child who he or she would like to pray for this week. Maybe it's someone at school, on a sports team, or in the neighborhood. Give them time to think of this person without making suggestions. God speaks to kids too! Talk about a time when God has answered prayers. Spend time as a family praying together. Look for ways God answers and celebrate together Pray on the way to school, to activities, or as you drive in and out of the neighborhood. Neighboring is a family affair!

LYNN'S STORY: LIVING A KAIROS LIFE

I rely heavily upon the Lord to direct activities. I purposefully try not to make things happen but to seek the Lord. It's called living a kairos life, which means living by opportunities that God creates as opposed to trying to making something happen. The apostle Paul wrote, "Be very careful, then, how you live—not as unwise but as wise, making the most of every opportunity" (Ephesians 5:15–16). I used to interpret that passage as meaning not to squander any of your time but really he is saying to be alert to what God is doing and the opportunities he presents to you. This connects with what Jesus said in John 5, "I only do what I see the Father doing." I can do nothing by myself. Jesus does it with the Father, and that's the same thing he invites us to. It's been a revelation to me to live that way, in interactions with both believers and nonbelievers. I have found three things that enable me to live life free of performance and trying to make something happen, allowing me to see what the Father is doing and joining him.

- **I pray**: Each Tuesday morning I walk through my neighborhood and pray for each of my neighbors by name. I ask the Lord to show me what he is doing in their lives. He has faithfully and dramatically shown me that he is in favor of my weekly prayer walks.

- **I wait**: Rather than try to make something happen in my neighborhood, after I pray, I wait for him. This is not passive, but waiting with a sense of expectation.

- **I watch**: Out of nowhere something will happen. A neighbor will call and ask me to perform a wedding or officiate a funeral. A fifty-foot tree blown down in front of our house opens opportunities with a neighbor. You can't make these kinds of situations happen. Because of his sovereign working and prayer, God has invited me to join what he is doing.

—Lynn Cory, California

prepare for next week

Prior to the next group meeting, read the
Week 4 introduction on your own before
the meeting.

"Who we have around our table says a lot about the Jesus we follow."
—Deb Hirsch

week 4:
play

start by connecting

1. What's your favorite hobby, sport or activity?

2. Share how last week's challenge went. What did you learn about yourself or someone else through that challenge? Where did you see God in your neighborhood this past week?

Hospitality

When play is activated in the way you neighbor another key element emerges—hospitality. As Rick shares in the video, hospitality comes from two Greek words: phileo and xenos. Phileo means friendship or brother. Xenos means stranger or foreigner. Hospitality is the ability to help a stranger feel like family. There's something about opening your door and welcoming people that sets the table for fun. As you sit around couches with drinks, or gather at a table with a delicious meal, or maybe hang out in the yard with some barbeque, something changes. Friends start to become family.

Your hospitality opens the door for stories to be told, jokes to be shared, and dreams to be revealed. Granted, those conversations may not always be fun and playful. Sometimes sad stories are shared and hurts are revealed. However, you hardly get to those deeper conversations without the light-hearted conversations. Opening your home can make that happen.

Our Most Unused Kingdom Resource

Our homes are the most underutilized physical resource in the kingdom. Pastors preach about being good stewards of time, talent, and treasure. A home is a big piece of the treasure. What if all the kitchens, back porches, grills, garages, tools, guest bedrooms, bathrooms, and kitchen tables were available for use in the kingdom?

What stops us from inviting people into our homes more? Could it be that Pinterest, HGTV or Better Homes and Gardens have raised our standard of hospitality to a level never intended by God? Having nice things, or wanting a nice home is not bad, but if everything has to be perfect in order for people to receive an invitation into our homes, we might be missing the point of hospitality altogether.

Scruffy Hospitality

Jack King captured the spirit of hospitality with a great nickname: scruffy hospitality. Here is what he means by that:

Scruffy hospitality means you're not waiting for everything in your house to be in order before you host and serve friends in your home. Scruffy hospitality means you hunger more for good conversation and serving a simple meal of what you have, not what you don't have. Scruffy hospitality means you're more interested in quality conversation than the impression your home or lawn makes. If we only share meals with friends when we're excellent, we aren't truly sharing life together.

Don't allow a to-do list to disqualify you from an evening with people you're called to love in friendship. Scheduling is hard enough in our world. If it's eating with kind, welcoming people in a less than perfect house versus eating alone, what do you think someone would choose? We tell our guests "come as you are," perhaps we should tell ourselves "host as you are." [4]

Hospitality and Our Spiritual Growth

Robert Lupton tells the story of an older woman in his community and his church. She had mild mental disabilities, was overweight, and had hygiene issues. With great authenticity and vulnerability, Lupton admits he was hesitant to invite her to his home, though she hinted on more than one occasion she would like to share Sunday dinner with them. His fear? That she would want to sit in his new recliner. To invite Mrs. Smith into their home meant for certain there would be soil and offensive odors. Lupton wrote:

Why should it be such a struggle to decide which is more godly: to welcome Mrs. Smith into my home and my corduroy recliner or to preserve the homey aroma of my sanctuary and get extra years of service from my furniture? Is this not precisely the issue of serving mammon or God? I thank God for Mrs. Smith and the conflict she brings me. In her, more clearly than in Sunday School lessons or sermons, I encounter the Christ of Scripture saying, "Inasmuch as you have done it unto the least of these brethren, you have done it unto me." [5]

Let Go and Have Fun

If you're not having fun, you're not doing it quite right. Good neighbors have fun together! And yes, Christians, can have fun. In fact, we SHOULD be having it. Pastor Ben Cachairas writes:

> "Play is something human beings were created to do! One intense perfectionist had a tendency to take herself too seriously. But God has been upending her outlook by telling her to 'lighten up.' God has told me the same thing. And God has used play to tell me.

> "Christians are famous for being all-business, un-fun people. I'd swear some believers I've met were baptized in lemon juice, based on the sour look on their faces."

> In stark contrast theologian Robert Hotchkins insists: "Christians ought to be celebrating constantly. We ought to be preoccupied with parties, banquets, feasts, and merriment. We ought to give ourselves over to veritable orgies of joy because of our belief in resurrection. We ought to attract people to our faith quite literally by the fun there is in being a Christian." [6]

And our fun can be simple and spontaneous. In the first week of December, Drew and his wife wanted to find a casual way to connect with their neighbors. As their family kicked around ideas, s'mores and hot cocoa came into the conversation. The upcoming Sunday night was free on the calendar, so they threw together ten simple handwritten invitations and included a graham cracker, a small chocolate bar, and a marshmallow in a bag.

Drew shares what happened next:

"Over the next few days we tried to catch our neighbors. We left the invitations on the doorsteps of those we missed. To be honest, we weren't optimistic that anyone would come. The weather forecast for that evening was quite cold, and it had snowed a couple of days earlier.

"That Sunday evening we backed the cars out of the garage, moved the fire pit to the center of the driveway, and set up a folding table. After the cocoa was heated and all the s'mores goodies had been laid out, we lit the fire and waited.

"Within minutes our neighbors began arriving. As each neighbor arrived, we welcomed them and introduced them to the other neighbors who had arrived. It was surprising how many of them did not know each other. A couple had recently moved in, but most just simply had not met.

"Over the course of an hour nearly all of neighbors joined in and enjoyed a s'more or cup of cocoa. While it was great to connect with our neighbors at Christmas, what most surprised us was how this easy gathering allowed us to introduce our neighbors to one another. We are growing in our love for our neighbors, and now our neighbors are growing in their relationship with each other."

The practice of PLAY in loving our neighbors is often overlooked and at times completely dismissed. The fear of what people will think of us sometimes drives us away from having a good time with the people around us. The Bible says that Jesus was not one to worry about that. He came eating and drinking and spent a great deal of time with people that the religious elite would frown upon. Jesus knew, however, that light belongs in dark places. He knew that love belonged where there was no love. Bottom line, neighbors practice PLAY. May God bless you with freedom to interact with your neighbors in ways that are fun!

watch the video

As a group, watch the short video teaching segments and take notes in the space provided below.

_____

_____

_____

_____

_____

_____

_____

_____

_____

_____

_____

_____

_____

scripture for foundation

Matthew 9:9-13

As Jesus went on from there, he saw a man named Matthew sitting at the tax collector's booth. "Follow me," he told him, and Matthew got up and followed him.

While Jesus was having dinner at Matthew's house, many tax collectors and sinners came and ate with him and his disciples. When the Pharisees saw this, they asked his disciples, "Why does your teacher eat with tax collectors and sinners?"

On hearing this, Jesus said, "It is not the healthy who need a doctor, but the sick. But go and learn what this means: 'I desire mercy, not sacrifice.' For I have not come to call the righteous, but sinners."

Isaiah 6:8

Then I heard the voice of the Lord saying, "Whom shall I send? And who will go for us?"

And I said, "Here am I. Send me!"

Philippians 2:19-20

I hope in the Lord Jesus to send Timothy to you soon, that I also may be cheered when I receive news about you. I have no one else like him, who will show genuine concern for your welfare.

Matthew 11:19

The Son of Man came eating and drinking, and they say, 'Here is a glutton and a drunkard, a friend of tax collectors and sinners.' But wisdom is proved right by her deeds."

questions for conversation

1. How do you think PLAY could be a powerful aspect of building relationships in your neighborhood?

    _____

    _____

    _____

2. Jesus' primary mode of "play" was eating with people. Examine Luke 5 below, and look for all the times Jesus was eating, around a table, or feeding people.

    One day as Jesus was standing by the Lake of Gennesaret, the people were crowding around him and listening to the word of God. He saw at the water's edge two boats, left there by the fishermen, who were washing their nets. He got into one of the boats, the one belonging to Simon, and asked him to put out a little from shore. Then he sat down and taught the people from the boat.

    When he had finished speaking, he said to Simon, "Put out into deep water, and let down the nets for a catch."

    Simon answered, "Master, we've worked hard all night and haven't caught anything. But because you say so, I will let down the nets."

When they had done so, they caught such a large number of fish that their nets began to break. So they signaled their partners in the other boat to come and help them, and they came and filled both boats so full that they began to sink.

When Simon Peter saw this, he fell at Jesus' knees and said, "Go away from me, Lord; I am a sinful man!" For he and all his companions were astonished at the catch of fish they had taken, and so were James and John, the sons of Zebedee, Simon's partners.

Then Jesus said to Simon, "Don't be afraid; from now on you will fish for people." So they pulled their boats up on shore, left everything and followed him.

While Jesus was in one of the towns, a man came along who was covered with leprosy. When he saw Jesus, he fell with his face to the ground and begged him, "Lord, if you are willing, you can make me clean."

Jesus reached out his hand and touched the man. "I am willing," he said. "Be clean!" And immediately the leprosy left him.

Then Jesus ordered him, "Don't tell anyone, but go, show yourself to the priest and offer the sacrifices that Moses commanded for your cleansing, as a testimony to them."

Yet the news about him spread all the more, so that crowds of people came to hear him and to be healed of their sicknesses. But Jesus often withdrew to lonely places and prayed.

One day Jesus was teaching, and Pharisees and teachers of the law were sitting there. They had come from every village of Galilee and from Judea and Jerusalem. And the power of the Lord was with Jesus to heal the sick. Some men came carrying a paralyzed man on a mat and tried to take him into the house to lay him before Jesus. When they could not find a way to do this because of the crowd, they went up on the roof and lowered him on his mat through the tiles into the middle of the crowd, right in front of Jesus.

When Jesus saw their faith, he said, "Friend, your sins are forgiven."

The Pharisees and the teachers of the law began thinking to themselves, "Who is this fellow who speaks blasphemy? Who can forgive sins but God alone?"

Jesus knew what they were thinking and asked, "Why are you thinking these things in your hearts? Which is easier: to say, 'Your sins are forgiven,' or to say, 'Get up and walk'? But I want you to know that the Son of Man has authority on earth to forgive sins." So he said to the paralyzed man, "I tell you, get up, take your mat and go home." Immediately he stood up in front of them, took what he had been lying on and went home praising God. Everyone was amazed and gave praise to God. They were filled with awe and said, "We have seen remarkable things today."

After this, Jesus went out and saw a tax collector by the name of Levi sitting at his tax booth. "Follow me," Jesus said to him, and Levi got up, left everything and followed him.

Then Levi held a great banquet for Jesus at his house, and a large crowd of tax collectors and others were eating with them. But the Pharisees and the teachers of the law who belonged to their sect complained to his disciples, "Why do you eat and drink with tax collectors and sinners?"

Jesus answered them, "It is not the healthy who need a doctor, but the sick. I have not come to call the righteous, but sinners to repentance."

They said to him, "John's disciples often fast and pray, and so do the disciples of the Pharisees, but yours go on eating and drinking."

Jesus answered, "Can you make the friends of the bridegroom fast while he is with them? But the time will come when the bridegroom will be taken from them; in those days they will fast."

He told them this parable: "No one tears a piece out of a new garment to patch an old one. Otherwise, they will have torn the new garment, and the patch from the new will not match the old. And no one pours new wine into old wineskins. Otherwise, the new wine will burst the skins; the wine will run out and the wineskins will be ruined. No, new wine must be poured into new wineskins. And no one after drinking old wine wants the new, for they say, 'The old is better.'"

3. Spend a few minutes talking about the power of meals. Why do you think that meals build meaningful bridges to friendship?

_____

_____

_____

4. What other ways can you engage in play with your neighbors?

_____

_____

_____

a. What can you invite them into (interests or hobbies of your own)?

_____

_____

_____

b. What can you join them in (interests and hobbies of theirs)?

_____

_____

_____

5. What does it take from us to have a lifestyle that is open for socializing with your neighbors?

_____

_____

_____

6. Jesus spent time with people that were not like him. What are the best ways to move into people's lives who may not be like you spiritually, politically, morally or financially?

_____

_____

_____

7. What is the scariest part of the practice of PLAY in loving your neighbor?

_____

_____

8. How can we overcome the fears of engagement?

_____

_____

_____

challenge for growth

Choose one challenge from this section to try out this week. Remember, you will report back to the group next week.

Find a way to PLAY this week, or at least start making the plan! Did you know there are 90 possible meals over the next month? Or here's another idea: bring your neighbor along with you! One of the best things about play is that you get to do the things you love. Do you love to garden? Garden with your neighbors! Do you love to bike, hike or dance? What if you asked your neighbor to join you? Those are just some ideas to get you started.

- **Crawl** : Pick one meal or activity to share with a neighbor. Write it here: _____

- **Walk** : Throw a Party! Put a date on the calendar and invite neighbors to a potluck, bbq or maybe get others involved and have a progressive dinner.

- **Run** : Make a commitment to devote 10% your meals over the next month to connecting with neighbors. What if one meal a week was dedicated to loving God by loving your neighbors, feeding them and offering hospitality?

prayer for strength

Pray for each other in the areas of margin (creating time for neighbors), flexibility, adaptability, love for neighbor, courage, initiative, intentionality and fun. When we get to the part in our loving our neighbor life that demands time and sacrifice and availability and resources, it really puts us at a crossroads of love. Spend time praying for each other. Spend time sharing a bit of your fears and simply asking God to release you of those fears. May God give you a playful spirit.

family on mission

Getting your family and neighbors to serve together is a great way to connect. Find out what the needs at the local food pantry are and your family could organize and host a food drive. Kids are great at helping with this. Go door to door handing out the list of most needed items and tell people your family will be back in a week to collect donations if they would like to participate. Pull the little red wagon out of the garage and go do the collection! To learn more tips about neighboring and serving together in this way you can visit www.canninghunger.org

ALAN'S STORY: FREE COFFEE FRIDAY

Free. Coffee. Friday. These are three of my favorite words, but if you put them together I get a little bit giddy. For the past four school years Fridays have catapulted us out of bed and back into neighborhood life. For about an hour each Friday morning we gather around caffeine and conversation with neighbors, bus drivers and school parents. As we sip on black gold we are reminded we are human. We are tired. We need to vent. We need to celebrate. We are wired for community. The coffee is mediocre; the connection is amazing. As a borderline coffee snob I've tried using the freshest locally roasted coffee in my city. These folks were raised on Folgers, so they aren't having it. Regular coffee from the grocery store will do the trick.

Once upon a time this was just a crazy idea. We had no clue if people would join us. We took a risk, threw out a sign, set up a card table, and waited. At first people had excuses of places to go and things to do. Shortly after "it clicked". Not only did people start drinking coffee with us; it became a community, a refuge for weary travelers through this crazy life. It's a space to pause, reconnect, fuel up for the day and celebrate the "already, not yet" of the weekend. [7]

This is bigger than caffeine.

—Alan Briggs, Colorado

prepare for next week

Prior to the next group meeting, read the
Week 5 introduction on your own before
the meeting.

How beautiful on the mountains are the feet of those who bring good news, who proclaim peace, who bring good tidings, who proclaim salvation, who say to Zion, 'Your God reigns!'"
Isaiah 52:7

week 5:
say

start by connecting

1. What is the funniest story you've ever heard? Have a couple of group members share their stories with the group.

2. Share how last week's challenge went. What did you learn about yourself or someone else through that challenge? Where did you see God in your neighborhood this past week?

Your Story. God's Story.

The practice of SAY is about story: your story and God's story. Almost always Jesus knew other people's stories before they heard his story. In the practice of SAY, you work hard to be present, aware of your neighbor's names, hopes and dreams. In SAY, your job is to share yours. Sharing our lives takes a significant amount of vulnerability and authenticity. SAY is about sharing faith, because it's a part of your life. But, here's where we've gotten evangelism all wrong.

We have thought of ourselves as salespeople when we're actually satisfied customers. We need to equip and empower one another to share the story of what God has done in our lives rather than what he's going to do for our neighbor. Consider the difference between these two phrases:

1. If you buy this car, you are going to love it!

2. I bought this car and I love it.

Which is the better approach? Number 2 of course. It has much more credibility. A lot of people would be more relaxed and relieved knowing they don't have to sell Jesus. We don't have to be traditional evangelists. Carl Medearis observed, "When we preach Christianity, we have to own it. When we preach Jesus, we don't have to own anything. Jesus owns us. We don't have to defend him. We don't even have to explain him. All we have to do is point with our fingers, like the blind man in the book of John, and say, 'There is Jesus. All I know is that he touched me, and where I was once blind, now I see.'" [8]

Being effective at sharing Jesus with others means living out faith with a motive of love, listening well, and having the courage to share our own lives. We don't have to worry about the results. God is going to take care of that. I plant, someone else waters, and God gives the increase. Robert Louis Stevenson wrote, "Don't judge each day by the harvest you reap but by the seeds that you plant." [9] Just love people. Don't try to win them.

The Jesus Way

Scripture offers a helpful passage on sharing faith. There are six lessons from Jesus in his interaction with the Samaritan woman (often called the Woman at the Well) recorded in John 4.

1. Jesus crossed barriers to meet people on their own turf. He crossed social, gender, and religious barriers because all of that was insignificant compared to the woman's soul. If you follow Jesus into personal evangelism, he will likely bring you into conflict with evangelical culture. John 4:4-9 says,

   Now he had to go through Samaria. So he came to a town in Samaria called Sychar, near the plot of ground Jacob had given to his son Joseph. Jacob's well was there, and Jesus, tired as he was from the journey, sat down by the well. It was about noon.

   When a Samaritan woman came to draw water, Jesus said to her, "Will you give me a drink?" (His disciples had gone into the town to buy food.)

   The Samaritan woman said to him, "You are a Jew and I am a Samaritan woman. How can you ask me for a drink?" (For Jews do not associate with Samaritans.)

2. Jesus used natural conversation to talk about spiritual topics. John 4:10-14 says,

   Jesus answered her, "If you knew the gift of God and who it is that asks you for a drink, you would have asked him and he would have given you living water."

   "Sir," the woman said, "you have nothing to draw with and the well is deep. Where can you get this living water? Are you greater than our father Jacob, who gave us the well and drank from it himself, as did also his sons and his livestock?"

   Jesus answered, "Everyone who drinks this water will be thirsty again, but whoever drinks the water I give them will never thirst. Indeed, the water I give them will become in them a spring of water welling up to eternal life."

Why did Jesus describe salvation as living water? Because they were already talking about water, so he just spiritualized it. Everyday, common events are springboards into the gospel. You can use natural conversation to talk about spiritual topics with your neighbors.

3. If Jesus saw that his approach, his conversation wasn't working, he didn't force it. Read what happens next in his conversation with the woman in John 4:15-16

   The woman said to him, "Sir, give me this water so that I won't get thirsty and have to keep coming here to draw water." He told her, "Go, call your husband and come back."

   Jesus saw she wasn't understanding, so he changed the subject. Not every conversation we have is going to be amazing. Don't sweat it.

4. Jesus focused on her life. John 4:17–18 says,

   "I have no husband," she replied. Jesus said to her, "You are right when you say you have no husband. The fact is, you have had five husbands, and the man you now have is not your husband. What you have just said is quite true."

   Learn your neighbors' histories, hopes, and hurts. If you listen to people, they will tell you how to reach them.

5. Jesus gently corrected her misunderstanding. If your neighbors misunderstand things about Jesus, faith, church or Christianity, it's okay to gently correct them. Look at how Jesus corrected her (John 4:19-24):

   "Sir," the woman said, "I can see that you are a prophet. Our ancestors worshiped on this mountain, but you Jews claim that the place where we must worship is in Jerusalem." "Woman,"

Jesus replied, "believe me, a time is coming when you will worship the Father neither on this mountain nor in Jerusalem. You Samaritans worship what you do not know; we worship what we do know, for salvation is from the Jews. Yet a time is coming and has now come when the true worshipers will worship the Father in the Spirit and in truth, for they are the kind of worshipers the Father seeks. God is spirit, and his worshipers must worship in the Spirit and in truth."

6. Jesus pointed toward himself as whom she needed. John 4:25–26 says,

    The woman said, "I know that Messiah" (called Christ) "is coming. When he comes, he will explain everything to us."

    Then Jesus declared, "I, the one speaking to you—I am he."

    Don't get distracted by tangents—cultural hot topics, historical black eyes (such as the Inquisition), etc.—keep bringing the conversation back to Jesus.

Help Your Neighbors See God

When you show people where God is working and moving, and when you point towards Jesus, you are creating God-awareness. You are opening up people's hearts and minds to the reality of God around them and a relationship with Jesus is real to you. That's ministry! When people start seeing God around them they have an opportunity to engage and participate with God himself. The idea is that we as Christians become signposts for God. We are not supposed to be God to people, but we can continue to point to him and his Son.

Sharing God's Story

There are four elements of God's story to consider as you talk to your neighbors about God.

CREATION - God created humans and everything on earth. It was all good. At the beginning humans had a loving and perfect relationship with God. Humans were to be God's image-bearers, be with him, and take care of all creation.

FALL - Humans (Adam and Eve) decided to go their own way by disobeying God's only command. This sin has followed humankind ever since, severing our relationship with God because God is holy and cannot allow evil to remain in his presence.

REDEMPTION- God did not want our relationship with him to remain broken. So he sent Jesus his son to repair the relationship. Jesus lived a sinless life, then died on the cross (taking on the punishment for all humanity's sin). He was raised to life again three days later conquering sin and death and offering us reconciliation with God.

RESTORATION - God invites us to join him in making all things right again. He will ultimately complete this work when he returns. At that time all things will be restored to the original beauty of creation and maybe even beyond—no more death, loss, tears, sin or darkness. Peace and love will reign with King Jesus.

Motives Matter

As Brian shares on the video, it is critical that we embrace the right motives when it comes to loving our neighbors:

OUR DEEPEST MOTIVE IS LOVE OUR HIGHEST HOPE IS FAITH.

We have to make sure that our motives and hopes are set in the right place because it is so easy for us to get them out of whack. Here's another way to think about it: We don't love people to make them Christian. We love people because we are Christian.

You see, although our deepest hope is for people to find faith in Christ and take part in all of the blessings of the Gospel, our motive is first and foremost love. Christians love people because Jesus loved people. We can help people realize that God is with them and that God is for them. Eugene Peterson paraphrased John 1:14 in this way: "The word became flesh and blood, and moved into the neighborhood."

watch the video

As a group, watch the short video teaching segments and take notes in the space provided below.

_____

_____

_____

_____

_____

_____

_____

_____

_____

_____

_____

_____

_____

scripture for foundation

1 Thessalonians 2:8

So we cared for you. Because we loved you so much, we were delighted to share with you not only the gospel of God but our lives as well.

2 Corinthians 5:21

God made him who had no sin to be sin for us, so that in him we might become the righteousness of God.

Acts 1:8

But you will receive power when the Holy Spirit comes on you; and you will be my witnesses in Jerusalem, and in all Judea and Samaria, and to the ends of the earth.

Colossians 4:5-6

Be wise in the way you act toward outsiders; make the most of every opportunity. Let your conversation be always full of grace, seasoned with salt, so that you may know how to answer everyone.

questions for conversation

1. In Acts 17:18, we learn, "Paul was preaching the good news about Jesus and the resurrection." And in Acts 20:24, good news is described as "the good news of God's grace." What does it mean to be good news to people?

    _____

    _____

    _____

2. What does it mean to tell the good news or to share the Gospel with people? Turn to the person on your right and say, "Jesus died for your sins." Then, turn to the person on your left and say, "Your sins are forgiven when you accept Jesus as your Savior." That's the good news!

    _____

    _____

    _____

3. Even Peter, one of Jesus' closest followers, denied knowing him (see Luke 22:54-60) Why is it so difficult sometimes to share your faith?

    _____

    _____

4. How can we overcome our fears? (See Acts 1:8 above)

_____

_____

_____

_____

5. What do you think is the best approach to sharing your life and your story of faith with people? (See Colossians 4:5-6 above)

_____

_____

_____

_____

6. Think about your neighbors. What are some natural ways to build bridges to a faith conversation?

_____

_____

_____

challenge for growth

Choose one challenge from this section to try out this week. Remember, you will report back to the group next week.

Spend time reflecting on how you came to know Jesus and accepted him as Lord and Savior. Also spend time reflecting on how you have felt blessed by God, when you have felt comforted by God and how you see God work in your life: past and present. Your faith story is a conversion story AND a continuing story. When you do have opportunity to share your story and God's story, share your story as a gift. Remember that you don't have to share your story all at one time. Let the story leak out of you little by little.

- **Crawl** : Work on your faith story. You can write it down, draw it, or create a timeline.
- **Walk** : Practice sharing your faith story with a friend, family member or another neighbor of faith. If you have another neighbor of faith, ask them to pray with you about sharing your story.
- **Run** : Start a book club. Whatever you and your neighbors choose to read, it will most likely lead you into conversations about life, love, conflict, resolution, good and evil. Those conversations can help you get to know your neighbors as well as stretch your own convictions about faith.

prayer for strength

Pray for each other in the areas of courage, confidence, being good news, and sharing our stories. Pray that God will fill our mouths with the right words that will explain well the beautiful news of Jesus to our neighbors. Pray that God gives us the wisdom to know when the right times are to share. Pray that God will open doors that are obvious to us. Pray that God prepares the hearts of our neighbors. May God bless you richly in allowing your stories of faith to flow freely from your lips.

family on mission

Where did you see God today? That simple question at the dinner table or before bed-time prayers can spark great conversations and build an awareness of God. Share your own faith story with your kids. Ask your kids how they would share God's story with others. Allow your faith to grow with each other as you keep your eyes open to share your faith with neighbors.

DRUE & LAURA'S STORY: WE ARE ALL BROKEN.

We had new neighbors that moved in right next door to us. My wife, Laura, and I have sought to get to know them and become friends. If he's out mowing the lawn and I am out there, I will ask him if he wants to have something cold to drink, then we watch kids play— simple stuff. We have intentionally NOT invited them to church or initiated spiritual conversation, we are just trying to develop some relationship.

I was outside making a phone call to a couple whose marriage was in crisis. I just ended the call when the wife next door came out with her one-year-old and started pulling weeds. She greeted me with, "Hey Drue, how are you? Working from home?"

I said, "Yeah, as long as I have a computer and phone I can pretty much work anywhere." I walked over toward her and just happened to mention that the last phone call I made was tough, a marriage was in crisis. I then said, "You know, we all struggle in some area or another. I've come to learn we are all broken, and we all struggle."

She started to break down and told me, "I just found out yesterday that my mom was diagnosed with a terminal disease." About that same time, Laura came out of the house and saw us. God opened such an unbelievable door for us to pray for her and love on her. She called her husband in that very moment and told him how God worked this out for her.

Since then, our friendship has grown, we've continued to have great conversations, they've asked for help in trying to find a church home, and he comes regularly to our neighborhood men's group. I think all this has happened just because we've loved them, we've been available, and we've been attentive to what's going on in their lives. Plus, they like us (at least we think so)! [10]

—Drue & Laura Warner, Georgia

prepare for next week

Prior to the next group meeting, read the
Week 6 introduction on your own before
the meeting.

"I am the Way and the Truth and the Life."
—Jesus

week 6:
a neighboring
way of life

start by connecting

1. If you could quit doing one thing right now, what would it be? (Think of errands, small tasks, or time wasters).

2. Share how last week's challenge went. What did you learn about yourself or someone else through that challenge? Where did you see God in your neighborhood this past week?

People of the Way

The early followers of Christ were called by numerous names. Some names they gave themselves and others were given to them. Jesus called them disciples and followers. The word "Christians" was first recorded in Acts 11:26: "The disciples were called Christians first at Antioch."

As Rick points out on the video, "The Way" is also mentioned several times throughout the book of Acts, starting with Luke's recounting of Saul's conversion: "He went to the high priest and asked him for letters to the synagogues in Damascus, so that if he found any there who belonged to the Way, whether men or women, he might take them as prisoners to Jerusalem" (9:1–2). This title likely goes back to Jesus' words in John 14:6: "I am the way and the truth and the life. No one comes to the Father except through me."

Inagrace Dietterich said this about the people of the Way:

> "The early followers of Jesus were not called people of 'the experience,' or the people of 'right doctrine,' or the people of 'moral values,' or even the people of 'the church.' They were called the people of 'the Way.' They were known for the way they lived, not only for what they believed or valued. Christians were associated with a particular and discernible way of living and relating that both grew out of their faith and gave testimony to that faith. More than just individuals who had a changed religious position, they were now a new people, a new community embarking on a new way of life—a life worthy of their calling. Their proclamation that in Jesus the reconciling and transforming reign of God had become a historical reality was more than an intriguing idea, it had become visible in a people whose life together was the first fruit of the new social order intended by God for the whole of creation." [11]

Being people of the Way gives the connotation that something was clearly different about them. The early Christians weren't giving up their freedoms or their lives for a doctrine, an ideology, or an organization. They were following a person who was the way, the truth, and the life. A resurrected and serving Messiah transformed everything.

The Neighboring Way of Life—Plus 1

Jesus lived a life of love and his greatest hope was that we would as well. His way of life can't be reduced to a worship service on Sunday. He firmly believed that his way of life should take over every fiber of our beings. Loving God and loving our neighbors wasn't meant to be a program, an initiative, or an event, it was meant to be a way of life. As we become people of "The Way of Jesus," we should start seeing the same patterns and rhythms of Jesus' life fleshed out in our own life. This new way of life is not about perfection; it's about trajectory. Get yourself on the path. Stay on the path. Do this one step at a time—with every step moving toward and in the ways of Jesus.

Kevin shared a story about missionaries in the Middle East struggling to find encouragement to continue their mission. With so little fruit from their work, they were discouraged. In an attempt to bolster their spirits, they decided to count everything they did in love toward their friends and neighbors. If someone made eye contact with them it was a Plus 1. If they were able to share a cup of tea — Plus 1. If there was a conversation, a meal, an act of service, or any other kind of interaction made in love — Plus 1, Plus 1, Plus 1. The hope was that someday all the Plus-1's would add up and tip the scales toward meaningful and transformational encounters and movement.

In the same way, every act of love toward our neighbors is a Plus 1 for the Kingdom of God. We are partnering with God when we obey his Greatest Commandment and follow through on the practices of neighboring: STAY, PRAY, PLAY, and SAY. Everything counts, and we are asking God to tip the scales.

When we learn a name—Plus 1. When we help clean a yard—Plus 1. When we listen to a neighbor's struggles with their kids—Plus 1. When we share a story about our faith—Plus 1. Every Plus 1 matters.

Make Room for Relationships

"Hear, O Israel: The Lord our God, the Lord is one. Love the Lord your God with all your heart and with all your soul and with all your mind and with all your strength." The second is this: "Love your neighbor as yourself." There is no commandment greater than these. (Mark 12:28-31)

Do you catch what is most important here? It is clearly about relationships; our relationships with God and others. But our lives are packed, aren't they? They are filled up with hours at work, kids' activities and of course, there are the things we do with the church. Good luck trying to fit anything else in! But we must. We must make time for what Jesus said matters most. How in the world do we make room for the relationships that matter most -- with God and with people? Here are some practical ways to make more room for the things that really matter:

- **Quit something.** Think through all the things you do. Pick one thing to quit. It will be difficult to do but at some point, you have to control your schedule instead of letting your schedule control you. This is a great exercise in prioritizing. What is really most important in your life?

- **Start earlier.** Yep....make room by adding more time. It's amazing what you could do with just one extra hour every few days. Do an early coffee or breakfast with a new friend before work.

- **Don't waste your lunches.** Most of us have a lunch time. Don't lunch alone. Invite someone to come with you or invite someone over for lunch.

- **Keep alert.** When doing everyday tasks, like yardwork, or going to the mailbox, stay in tune with others around you. When a neighbor walks by take a break and create some room for them.

California State Professor and good neighbor, Don Simmons, summed up neighboring pretty well. He said, "If I am supposed to understand scripture and be like Jesus, then this is what Jesus would do. This is how Jesus lived. He was conscious of the people closest to him. He didn't leave them out. He was never too busy. If Christ-likeness is the goal, I can't obtain it without loving my neighbor."

Priesthood of Believers

Peter calls the church a holy nation and a priesthood of all believers. 1 Peter 2:9-10 says:

> *"But you are a chosen people, a royal priesthood, a holy nation, God's special possession, that you may declare the praises of him who called you out of darkness into his wonderful light. Once you were not a people, but now you are the people of God; once you had not received mercy, but now you have received mercy."*

We have been chosen and set apart by God to receive his mercy. It's a gift worth naming and claiming. It's a statement of fact and of hope. God's mercy should compel us to be light in the darkness. Peter also tells us that we are to live such good lives that though people may accuse you of doing wrong, they won't be able to deny the good works seen in you. Upon seeing Jesus in you, they will "glorify God on the day he visits us. (1 Peter 2:12). Can you imagine your life so markedly different and attractive because of Christ that people are drawn to God and glorify him? Being the best neighbor your neighbors have ever had could be the start! While it's just a street full of people that you are to spiritually care for and care about, our collective representation of Christ can change the city and change the world.

watch the video

As a group, watch the short video teaching segments and take notes in the space provided below.

_____

_____

_____

_____

_____

_____

_____

_____

_____

_____

_____

_____

_____

_____

scripture for foundation

John 1:14

The Word became flesh and made his dwelling among us. We have seen his glory, the glory of the one and only Son, who came from the Father, full of grace and truth.

1 Corinthians 3:16

Don't you know that you yourselves are God's temple and that God's Spirit dwells in your midst?

Philippians 2:13

For it is God who works in you to will and to act in order to fulfill his good purpose.

questions for conversation

1. Think about your rhythm and pattern of life. Have the group members pair up and share how a usual day goes for them. For example: "Get up. Get ready. Go to work. Eat lunch. Go back to work. Pick the kids up from school. Go home. Eat dinner. Work on homework. Get ready for bed. Put kids to bed. Read. Go to sleep. Do it again."

2. Beyond your actual rhythms, what are the guiding principles or values you live by? Name a few.

3. Ask for a volunteer to read the following passages:

Jesus gave them this answer: "Very truly I tell you, the Son can do nothing by himself; he can do only what he sees his Father doing, because whatever the Father does the Son also does. For the Father loves the Son and shows him all he does. Yes, and he will show him even greater works than these, so that you will be amazed. John 5:19-20

For I did not speak on my own, but the Father who sent me commanded me to say all that I have spoken. I know that his command leads to eternal life. So whatever I say is just what the Father has told me to say." John 12:49-50

Greater love has no one than this: to lay down one's life for one's friends. You are my friends if you do what I command. I no longer call you servants, because a servant does not know his master's business. Instead, I have called you friends, for everything that I learned from my Father I have made known to you. You did not choose me, but I chose you and appointed you so that you might go and bear fruit—fruit that will last—and so that whatever you ask in my name the Father will give you. This is my command: Love each other. John 15:13-17

For John the Baptist came neither eating bread nor drinking wine, and you say, 'He has a demon.' The Son of Man came eating and drinking, and you say, 'Here is a glutton and a drunkard, a friend of tax collectors and sinners.' But wisdom is proved right by all her children." Luke 7:33-35

Now the tax collectors and sinners were all gathering around to hear Jesus. Luke 15:1

4. Now think about Jesus. What was his way of life? What was his rhythm and pattern of life? What was his purpose? Together as a group try to piece together a robust picture of Jesus' way of life using the verses above to guide your conversation.

_____

_____

_____

5. From the verse above, what's different about Jesus' life when compared to your life? (Don't be too hard on yourself).

_____

_____

_____

6. 2 Peter 1:3 says, "His divine power has given us everything we need for a godly life through our knowledge of him who called us by his own glory and goodness." What has God's divine power given us? (Hint: 3 words)

_____

_____

7. What can we do to start shifting our way to his way?

_____

_____

_____

challenge for growth

Choose one challenge from this section to try out this week. Remember, you will report back to the group next week.

Pick one way you can shift from your patterns and rhythms to Jesus' patterns and rhythms. This is not about starting a quiet time or a Bible reading program. Think more about the actual way you are living your life. How can you make your way of life look more like the way of Jesus? Try one new way of living. At first it will feel hard or even unnatural. As you live this new pattern, notice how it changes you or even how it changes the way others react.

prayer for strength

Pray for each other in the areas of life change and transformation. Pray for continued open-heartedness toward the way God is trying to transform us and grow us. Pray for continued desire to be changed by God. Pray for courage to change. Pray for commitment to change. Pray for the way of Jesus to be more and more our way of living. Pray for the Holy Spirit's empowerment to live this new way of life.

family on mission

Just like adults have a rhythm for life, children do as well. As a family write down all the things you have going on—work, school, sports, friends, church, activities, etc. Talk about what is most important out of that list. Discuss what could change to allow for more time to love God and love others. During some seasons of life, you may not be able to add anything more to your schedule. If this is one of those times, think about ways that you could neighbor where you're at—your children's sport teams, connecting with your child's teacher, going out to ice cream with a family after a school concert, etc.

bonus neighboring tips

OBEY: From List to Lifestyle

Loving God and loving our neighbors as ourselves is not just a good idea. It is the proof that we are in Christ. Francis Chan writes:

"Following Jesus is not about diligently keeping a set of rules or conjuring up the moral fortitude to lead good lives. It's about loving God and enjoying Him...But lest we think that we can love God and live any way we want to, Jesus told us very clearly, 'If you love me, you will keep my commandments' (John 14:15). The love for God in the first commandment is made practical in the love for our neighbors in the second commandment. John actually told us that if we don't love the people that we can see around us, then we don't love God, whom we can't see (1 John 4:20)." [12]

Going through a study together like this one about neighboring is a good start, but how will you keep obeying this command of Christ? In this Greatest Commandment, Jesus is essentially asking us to double major: love God and love your neighbor. Most followers of Christ set aside Sunday mornings to worship and learn about God, drawing closer to him, and loving him. There's no calendar for neighboring...or could there be? Why not take 5 minutes and set weekly reminders on your phone for the next several months to pray for your neighbor or do something nice for your neighbor.

STAY: Don't Move.

Could loving our neighbors literally mean we stay in place long enough to show and share God's love? The average American moves once at least every five years. While a lot of people relocate for job reasons, many people are looking at a new house for the purpose of bigger and better or smaller and more manageable. Sometimes people move because the neighborhood isn't what it used to be. What if Christians were people who stayed, put down deeper roots?

What if we are willing to ask one another "How will this move affect not just your family, but your neighbors and community?"

While the Bible does include numerous accounts of people God asked to go, think of the thousands not recorded who likely stayed in place, even when the neighborhood went downhill. The early Christians were known as people who had staying power. When two plagues hit Rome, it was the Christians who stayed to take care of the sick and dying. When the Roman culture began abandoning their children born from unwanted pregnancies, the early Christians didn't run from the moral decay, they engaged in it. They went out at night and scoured the ditches, canals, and the areas outside the city walls where unwanted infants would be abandoned. They took the babies home and cared for them as their own children. What was the outcome to this "stay and engage" mode of operation? The early church grew...at the rate of 40 percent a month.

PRAY: Pray Like Jesus over Your Neighborhood
In Matthew 6:5-13 Jesus says,

> *"This, then, is how you should pray: 'Our Father in heaven, hallowed be your name, your kingdom come, your will be done, on earth as it is in heaven. Give us today our daily bread. And forgive us our debts, as we also have forgiven our debtors. And lead us not into temptation, but deliver us from the evil one.'"*

It only takes about 10 seconds to read that prayer and about 15 seconds to say it. What if we prayed the Lord's Prayer over our entire neighborhoods as well as our next door neighbors? We could pray for God's holiness to reside among us; for him to meet all the needs on our cul-de-sac; that our relationships as neighbors would be marked by forgiveness and grace; and that evil would stay away from our streets. It's a simple prayer that Jesus invited us to pray. It is applicable to our lives and our neighbor's lives every day.

PLAY: What Kind of Neighbor Are You?
Have some fun! Here are ten questions to help you see what kind of neighboring you really are.

1. I like my neighbors.

   Yes   Somewhat   **No**

2. My neighbors like me.

   Yes   Somewhat   **No**

3. I talk to my neighbors.

   Yes   Somewhat   **No**

4. I do nice things for my neighbors.

   Yes   Somewhat   **No**

5. I genuinely care about my neighbors.

   Yes   Somewhat   **No**

6. My neighbors invite me to their parties.

   Yes   Somewhat   **No**

7. I actually like going to my neighbor's parties.

   Yes   Somewhat   **No**

8. I know what's happening in my neighborhood.

   Yes   Somewhat   **No**

9. I watch out for my neighborhood.

   Yes   Somewhat   **No**

10. When people need help in my neighborhood, they come to me.

    Yes   Somewhat   **No**

Now tally your score: 2 points for every Yes, 1 point for every Somewhat, 0 points for every No.

What kind of neighbor are you?

- 17—20 points, Mr. Rogers: You are the best neighbor ever. You know your neighbors and you're engaged in your neighborhood.

- 13—16 points, Steve Urkel: You are a little quirky and sometimes annoying, but deep down you are good-hearted and always do the right thing.

- 9—12 points, Wilson: You are always there and are always willing to share friendly advice, but you like to stay on your side of the fence.

- 5—8 points, Ned Flanders: You're trying hard, but people are just not getting you.

- 0—4 points, Newman: Not sure who would like living next to you. You are in desperate need of some neighboring help.

SAY: Ask Better Questions

To have better conversations and share our lives, we need to ask better questions of each other and our neighbors. "What's your name?" "What do you do?" are good starting places but Jesus was always asking way more interesting questions than that. Here are some easy, but better follow up questions we can ask one another to get to know each other and share our own stories.

- How did you end up in _____ (insert your state or city)?

- What was your best day ever?

- Where did you grow up?

- What were some of your hobbies as a kid?

- What do you like to do for fun now?

- What's one of your dream vacations?

- How did you meet your wife/husband?

- What's one of the best gifts you've ever received?

one another

Verses highlighting the attitudes and actions we should have for one another.

- Love one another: John 13:34–35; 15:12, 17; Romans 12:10; 13:8; 14:13; 1 Thessalonians 3:12; 4:9; 2 Thessalonians 1:3 ; 1 Peter 1:22; 1 John 3:11, 22; 4:7, 11-12; 2 John 1:5

- Serve one another: Galatians 5:13, 21; Philippians 2:3; 1 Peter 4:9; 5:5

- Accept one another: Romans 15:7, 14

- Strengthen one another: Romans 14:19

- Help one another: Hebrews 3:13; 10:24

- Encourage one another: Romans 14:19; 15:14; Colossians 3:16; 1 Thessalonians 5:11; Hebrews 3:13; 10:24-25

- Care for one another: Galatians 6:2

- Forgive one another: Ephesians 4:32; Colossians 3:13

- Submit to one another: Ephesians 5:21; 1 Peter 5:5

- Commit to one another: 1 John 3:16

- Build trust with one another: 1 John 1:7

- Be devoted to one another: Romans 12:10

- Be patient with one another: Ephesians 4:2; Colossians 3:13

- Be interested in one another: Philippians 2:4

- Be accountable to one another: Ephesians 5:21

- Confess to one another: James 5:16

- Live in harmony with one another: Romans 12:16

- Do not be conceited to one another: Romans 13:8
- Do not pass judgment to one another: Romans 14:13; 15:7
- Do not slander one another: James 4:11
- Instruct one another: Romans 16:16
- Greet one another: Romans 16:16; 1 Corinthians 1:10; 2 Corinthians 13:12
- Admonish one another: Romans 5:14; Colossians 3:16
- Spur one another toward love and good deeds: Hebrews 10:24
- Meet with one another: Hebrews 10:25
- Agree with one another: 1 Corinthians 16:20
- Be concerned for one another: Hebrews 10:24
- Be humble to one another in love: Ephesians 4:2
- Be compassionate to one another: Ephesians 4:32
- Do not be consumed by one another: Galatians 5:14–15
- Do not anger one another: Galatians 5:26
- Do not lie to one another: Colossians 3:9
- Do not grumble to one another: James 5:9
- Give preference to one another: Romans 12:10
- Be at peace with one another: Romans 12:18
- Sing to one another: Ephesians 5:19
- Be of the same mind to one another: Romans 12:16; 15:5
- Comfort one another: 1 Thessalonians 4:18; 5:11
- Be kind to one another: Ephesians 4:32
- Live in peace with one another: 1 Thessalonians 5:13
- Carry one another's burdens: Galatians 6:2

appendices

leading for the first time

1. **Prepare.**

   As the leader of this group, you don't have to be the expert. The experts are on the video, so let the teaching lead the way. But, before the meeting, it's a good idea to review the video and the discussion questions yourself. The videos are only 10 minutes long, then just read through the questions.

   If you find your group doesn't have time to complete the entire discussion guide, that's ok. Prioritize the questions for the time you have available. As you get to know the group, choose questions that are appropriate for the group. If your group has been together for a while, or if your group members are well beyond the basics, then maybe skip the first Getting Started question, and go for the second question which is more of an accountability question regarding what they committed to do in the previous meeting.

2. **Pray for Your Group.**
   If you feel anxious about leading the group or even inadequate, that is perfectly normal, especially if you are leading for the first time. The Bible says, "Do not be anxious about anything, but in every situation, by prayer and petition, with thanksgiving, present your requests to God. And the peace of God, which transcends all understanding, will guard your hearts and your minds in Christ Jesus" (Philippians 4:6-7). So how often should you pray? Pray every time you feel anxious. God will give you peace.

   The video and discussion guide are pretty easy to use. It's practically a no brainer. But, just because the curriculum is easy to use, doesn't mean you should go into the meeting "cold" spiritually. Commit the meeting to God. Invite His presence into your meeting, then watch Him work.

3. **Guiding the Discussion.**
   While everyone should have a chance to share their thoughts and experiences, as the leader your job is to facilitate a discussion, not to teach a class. You want to make sure everyone gets their word in. You also want to make sure no one dominates the discussion. If someone tends to jump in on every question, politely say, "Now, on this next question let's hear from a few of you who haven't had a chance to share." If the person dominating the meeting continues to do this, then you might need to talk to them outside of the group meeting.

   Since you as the leader prepared ahead of time for the lesson, don't count on all of the group members preparing ahead for this meeting. When you ask the discussion questions, it may take the group members a couple of seconds to put their thoughts together. That's ok. Don't feel you as the leader need to fill the silence. Let them think a minute.

4. **Praying Together as a Group.**
    Habits are hard to break and sometimes hard to start. Changing a person's views and behaviors requires more than just willpower. It requires God's power. At the end of every meeting subgroup into groups of 3-4 people, so everyone can talk about their needs, and then pray together. In a large group, some people won't share, and it will take a much longer time, so sub-grouping is necessary.

    Also, limit the prayer requests to what is personally affecting the group member. Now, they may be concerned about Aunt Gertrude's big toe or something they read about on the internet, but this really isn't the place to discuss that. As much as you can keep the focus of the prayer time on the changes group members need to make.

5. **Ask for Volunteers.**
    Don't lead the group alone. Just because you are the designated leader, you do not need to do everything for the group. In fact, delegate as much as you possibly can: the refreshments, the home you meet in, and even leading the discussion. If you do this right, you might only need to lead for the first session, then others will lead for the rest.

    As group members become more involved in the leadership, they will feel a stronger sense of ownership in the group. Pretty soon the group will go from being "your group" to being "our group."

frequently asked questions

1. **How long should we plan for the meeting?**
   You should plan for a 90 minute to 2 hour meeting to allow
   for sufficient time for socializing, discussion, and prayer. Start
   your meeting on time, even if a few people are running late. By
   starting on time, the late group members will be apologetic and
   will figure out that the group is serious about starting on time.
   If you wait for them, then you are reinforcing their bad behavior.
   They will learn that the group will wait for them, so they don't
   need to show up until 15 minutes after the stated start time.

   You also want to end the meeting on time. If your group meets
   on a "school night," then parents will be anxious to get the
   children home and to bed -- not to mention they need to go to
   work in the morning. After the discussion and prayer time, let
   people know that if they need to go, then they are welcome to.
   But, if they'd like to stay, then they can do that also. This doesn't
   make it awkward for people if they need to get going.

2. **What if we don't cover all of the questions?**
   The goal of the group meeting is not to cover all of the
   questions, but to use the questions as a tool for facilitating the
   group discussion. As the group leader, take time before the
   meeting to pick out five or six questions which will be core to
   your group discussion. In each lesson, several questions have an
   asterisk by the key questions for the lesson. If you have time to
   get to the rest of the questions, feel free to do so, but don't feel
   obligated to ask and answer every question in the lesson.

3. **Should the leader ever interrupt a group member who is
   sharing something?**
   This is a tricky one that depends on what is being shared and
   why. If it's clear that the person is going down a rabbit trail,
   then you should redirect them when they take a breath. Say
   something like, "That's a very interesting thought, but we're
   going to have to save that discussion for another time" or "I'm

really interested in what you're saying, maybe we can continue that conversation after the meeting."

Be sensitive. If the group member is sharing something personal, you might want to give them some space to talk about what's on their heart. If this turns into a pattern every week, then you should redirect the discussion. If you're unsure about what to do, reach out to your coach or your small group pastor. Before you cut them off, say a quick prayer and ask for the Holy Spirit's guidance in how to handle the situation.

4. **Is it okay to serve alcoholic beverages in the group?**
Serving alcoholic beverages is really not a good idea in small group meetings. Since the church is a place where broken people come for healing, some of that brokenness centers around substance abuse. In the case of the small group, it's best to practice what the Bible says in 1 Corinthians 8 and abstain for the sake of others.

5. **How should the room be arranged?**
The furniture should be arranged so everyone in the group can see each other. Couches can be a challenge, in that, if three people are sitting on the couch, then the people on either end can't see each other. It's better to add more chairs than to create blind spots in the meeting room.

Also, groups do better meeting indoors rather than outdoors. Unless the group meeting is in a very remote location, meeting outdoors often stifles the discussion because group members are afraid of being overheard by the neighbors.

6. **What happens if the group is too big for the room?**
If your group is larger than eight people, you should subgroup for the discussion. This will not only make the seating arrangement more comfortable, but it will also allow everyone to get a word in. The group can crowd in to watch the video together, then break up into smaller groups for the discussion. You might even break into yet smaller groups of three or four people for the prayer time.

gathering a group

As you are starting your new group or adding to an existing group, the best place to start is to think about the people in your life who would enjoy a study like this. Some of those people may attend your church, but don't stop there. Think about all of your relationships: friends, neighbors, co-workers, relatives, and others. In fact, make a list of these folks and pray about inviting them to your group.

If you're stuck, then look at your cell phone. Who are the last 20 people you have called? Okay, you're probably not going to invite your dentist or your children's teachers, but you might. Your frequently called (or texted) numbers reveal the people you are in regular contact with. Put them on your prayer list too.

Then, pray. Pray about inviting the people who are on your list. And, prayer about people who are not on your list. Ask God who He would like for you to invite to your group, then pay attention to who crosses your path in the next few days. If you ask, God will bring people to your group.

But, don't stop with just your list. If you have a co-leader, ask him or her to create a list. As you invite people to your group, ask them who they would like to invite to the group.

Before you know it, you will have a room full of people ready to join you in the study.

group agreement

Our group agrees to meet together for six weeks beginning _____

(Date)

The group will meet every _____

(Day of Week)

from _____

(Start Time)

to _____

(End Time)

As a group, we value:

Confidentiality
Whatever is said in the group will be held in strictest confidence and will not be discussed outside of the group. Group members should also honor the confidentiality of others. When a member shares, they should only talk about their own lives, sinfulness, doubts, concerns, and worries and will not share any of these things for another group member or anyone outside the group.

Openness
Our group is a place to get real with each other. Good discussions can't be built on churchy answers. We aim to hit where the rubber meets the road. Group members are encouraged to be vulnerable, open up, and share their lives and experiences with the group.

Courtesy

We will not interrupt others when they are talking, but will wait for them to finish. We will also extend courtesy by making sure people feel heard. We will avoid quick fixes to anyone's issues or advice giving of any kind.

Staying on Topic

The group meetings are built around lessons. We ask that everyone's comments remain on topic during the group discussion time. We will stay away from controversial issues, politics, and rabbit trails in general. If the discussion gets off track, the group leader will redirect the discussion.

Group Attendance

Every group member is expected at every group meeting. If for some reason a group member is unable to attend, the member should contact the group leader to let them know about their absence before the group meeting.

Group Participation

This group is not just the leader's group. This is our group. Everyone is expected to take turns at leading the discussion, hosting in their home, leading the prayer time, bringing refreshments, or some other aspect of group leadership.

small group roster

NAME	EMAIL	CELL PHONE NUMBER

small group calendar

MEETING DATE	DISCUSSION LEADER	MEETING HOST	PRAYER LEADER	REFRESHMENTS

[1] Adapted from Lynn Cory, Neighborhood Initiative and the Love of God, (Lynn Cory, 2013), 107-109.

[2] Mike Snider, "Cocooning: It's back and thank to tech, it's bigger," USA Today, February 18, 2013, http://www.usatoday.com/story/tech/personal/2013/02/15/internet-tv-super-cocoons/1880473/ (accessed July 24, 2015).

[3] Alan Roxburgh, Moving Back into the Neighborhood: The Workbook (West Vancouver, BC: Alan Roxburgh, 2010), 29. See www.wichurches.org/sitecontent/pdf_files/programs/moving_back_into_neighborhood.pdf.

[4] Jack King, "Why Scruffy Hospitality Creates Space for Friendship," May 21, 2014, Knox Priest, http://www.knoxpriest.com/scruffy-hospitality-creates-space-friendship/ (accessed July 24, 2015).

[5] Robert Lupton, Theirs Is the Kingdom: Celebrating the Gospel in Urban America (New York: HarperCollins, 1989), 9.

[6] Ben Cachairas, "Thoughts on Play Part 1", June 12, 2014, http://outofmymind.cc/thoughts-on-play-part-i/ (accessed November 10, 2016).

[7] Alan Briggs, Sacred Gathering of Caffeine and Converstion, http://www.theneighboringchurch.com/blog/sacred-gathering-of-caffeine-conversation/ Alan talks more about free coffee Fridays in his book Staying is the new Going; Choosing to love where God places you.

[8] Carl Medearis, Speaking of Jesus: The Art of Not-Evangelism (Colorado Springs: David C. Cook, 2011), Kindle Edition, 47–48.

[9] Robert Louis Stevenson, www.brainyquote.com (accessed May 19, 2015).

[10] Learn more about the Warners decade of neighboring in Georgia in their 3 Part interview with Krista Petty, Meet the Warners, http://www.theneighboringchurch.com/blog/part-2-meet-the-warners-neighboring-all-in/

[11] Inagrace T. Dietterich, Cultivating Missional Communities (Eugene, OR: Wipf and Stock, 2006), 13.

[12] Chan, Frances Chan, Multiply: Disciples Making Disciples, (Colorado Springs, CO: David C Cook, 2012), 22.

about the authors

Brian Mavis is the President of America's Kids Belong and former Pastor of Community Transformation at LifeBridge Christian Church. Brian was the first General Manager of SermonCentral.com from 2000-2005. He has written curriculum for campaigns including Bono's *One Sabbath Campaign*, Mel Gibson's *Passion of the Christ*; World Vision's *Faith in Action* and *The Hole in Our Gospel*. Brian co-authored The Neighboring Church along with Rick Rusaw. Brian and his wife, Julie, have two daughters and reside in Windsor, CO.

Rick Rusaw is the Senior Pastor at LifeBridge Christian Church. He is co-author of several books including *The Neighboring Church, The Externally Focused Church, The Externally Focused Quest, The Externally Focused Life*, and the *Life on Loan* series. Prior to LifeBridge, Rick served as a Vice President at Cincinnati Christian University. Rick and his wife, Diane, have three children and five grandchildren and reside in Longmont, CO.

Kevin Colón is a pastor, coach, and mentor who has served in the Denver/Boulder area since 2002. Currently, Kevin works with GlocalNet, a group relentlessly pursuing peace and reconciliation among all peoples in all places for all things. Their work focuses on multi-faith collaborations, city and nations engagement and starting new churches. He is married to Amy and has three teenage daughters. Formerly, Kevin served as the Neighboring Life Pastor at LifeBridge Christian Church.

Krista Petty is a connector and story-teller for neighboring and community transformation movements across the U.S. She has served with Leadership Network, LifeBridge Christian Church, Carolina Cross Connection, Simon Solutions, and many others. Krista and her husband, Steve, live in Spirit Lake, IA and have three children and two grandsons.